FUNERAL AND MEMORIAL RITUALS IN THE POKUTTYA REGION (UKRAINE)

Ihor Halias

Lviv, Ukraine

2024

Abstract

Each of us eventually reaches a moment when we begin to contemplate the unknown depths of existence. Human beings, unique creatures, consciously acknowledge their limitations and become subjects of their own reflections on death. Death is considered an inseparable conclusion to life, its ultimate point. Funerals and memorial ceremonies are always filled with tragedy and sorrow due to the loss of loved ones. However, for relatives, this is the last opportunity to pay homage to the deceased.

The traditional funeral and memorial rituals of Ukrainians impress with their uniqueness and archaic nature, highlighting the ethnic identity and ancient roots of folk culture. Many of these archaisms can be observed in the customs of Hutsuls, Boykos, Lemkos, as well as in the traditions of the Pokutians. Observing these traditions is extremely important for understanding Ukrainian and, more broadly, Slavic antiquities. Folk funeral rites encompass pre-funeral, funeral, and post-funeral stages, incorporating memorial customs and rituals. An integral part is also the traditional beliefs and conceptions regarding death, the soul, and life after death.

The book «FUNERAL AND MEMORIAL RITUALS IN THE POKUTTYA REGION (UKRAINE)» is a bachelor's research conducted and defended by the author at Ivan Franko Lviv National University in 2023. (Lviv, Ukraine).

CONTENTS

INTRODUCTION

In everyone's life, there comes a moment, sooner or later, when one questions the finiteness of their existence. Humans are the only beings capable of realizing their mortality and contemplating it. Death is the deserved conclusion of life, its ultimate point. Undoubtedly, funerals and memorial services for people are always filled with grief, tragedy, and sorrow due to the loss of loved ones, but for relatives, it is the last chance to pay tribute to the departed.

The traditional funeral and memorial rituals of Ukrainians contain many unique and archaic ritualistic and ideological phenomena, demonstrating the ethnic distinctiveness and ancient roots of folk customs. There are particularly numerous archaisms in the customs and rituals of Hutsuls, Boykos, and Lemkos, but no less in those of the Pokuttya region. Therefore, studying their traditions is extremely important for understanding Ukrainian and, in general, Slavic antiquities.

The structure of the folk funeral ritual consists of pre-funeral, funeral, and post-funeral, namely memorial customs and rituals. Additionally, traditional beliefs and views about death, the soul, and the afterlife of a person are an integral part.

The relevance of the research lies in the fact that an increasing number of young people, and not only them, are becoming interested in the ethno-cultural heritage of the Ukrainian people. This interest is driven by the intensification of socio-national processes in Ukraine over the last decade. This curiosity has led to a thorough exploration of all key aspects of traditional folk culture and way of life. A particular focus in the study of Ukrainian antiquities is on the examination of family customs and rituals, as they are an integral part of every person's life. These customs are intricately linked to key events in the human life cycle and encompass many unique and ancient practices.

Some components of this segment of the spiritual culture of the people, such as childbirth and wedding customs and rituals, have already been illuminated in separate monographs. Regarding funeral rites, there are generalized historical and ethnographic works on Ukrainian funeral traditions and their ethno-local features in domestic ethnology, but their quantity is not as abundant as one would desire.

Therefore, the study of funeral rituals among Ukrainians, particularly their regional characteristics and specifics, is one of the urgent scientific tasks. Funeral customs, however bluntly it may sound, await us all, both as the main protagonist of this act and as its participants. Due to its exceptional conservatism, funeral ritualism preserves many relics of ancient Ukrainian culture. Its specialized study is relevant not only from the perspective of prospective directions in Ukrainian and Slavic studies but also in the fields of ethnogenesis, ritualistics, and cultural studies.

The study of the traditions of the population of the Ukrainian Carpathians is of utmost importance, as it is a region with well-preserved household and ritual archaic elements. These traditions have formed under the influence of the natural conditions of the mountainous terrain and are relatively resistant to change over time, constituting a valuable cultural heritage.

The object of the research is the analysis of funeral and memorial customs and rituals of the inhabitants of Pokuttia from the second half of the 19th century to the first half of the 20th century.

The subject of the research is the structural features of funeral and memorial customs and rituals of the inhabitants of Pokuttia from the second half of the 19th century to the first half of the 20th century.

The aim of the research is to identify historical and ethnographic features of funeral and memorial rituals of the inhabitants of Pokuttia from the second half of the 19th century to the first half of the 20th century.

To achieve the set goal, a series of tasks needs to be performed:

- Determine the contributions of Ukrainian ethnologists in this topic.

- Identify the geographical and chronological boundaries of funeral customs, rituals, and beliefs.

- Determine the main features of pre-funeral ritualism in Pokuttia.

- Analyze the main features of funeral ritualism.

- Identify memorial customs and rituals after burial.

- Analyze memorial motifs in the calendar.

- Trace the structural-functional features of the main components and attributes in pre-funeral, funeral, and memorial ritualism.

- Formulate conclusions for the research.

For the study of this topic, the historical-ethnographic region of Pokuttia was chosen. Additionally, since I have been researching funeral and memorial ritualism in the Ukrainian Carpathians for the past two years, this study will involve many comparisons between the customs and rituals of Pokuttia and those of the Boykos, Lemkos, and especially the Hutsuls. The Carpathians are where ancient customs and rituals are well-preserved, as they formed in the natural conditions of a mountainous region, which is difficult for the influence of other historical-ethnographic groups to penetrate. In this territory, the indigenous population of three historical-ethnographic regions of Ukraine resides – Boikivshchyna, Hutsulshchyna, and Lemkivshchyna. The funeral ritualism of the highlanders from the late 19th to the first half of the 20th century is considered in the entire massif of their compact settlement, including historical Ukrainian lands that are now within the borders of neighboring states. The functioning of funeral traditions in the second half of the 20th century and the beginning of the 21st century is primarily investigated based on data collected in mountainous areas of western regions of contemporary Ukraine.

The chronological boundaries of the study encompass the second half of the 19th century, specifically from the emergence of the first ethnographic descriptions of funeral ritualism in Pokuttia, concluding with the first half of the 20th century. In other words, we can confidently state that this research covers the contemporary period of the formation of folk traditions. The territorial and chronological boundaries were often expanded because it was deemed necessary to compare the traditions of Ukrainians in the Carpathians and Pokuttia with the overall Ukrainian tradition to trace the historical roots of such commonality.

A significant number of publications of various character and significance are devoted to funeral and memorial ritualism. Especially noteworthy are ethnographic studies, as ethnographic materials encompass the entire range of folk customs.

During the research, the work of Volodymyr Hnatiuk, «Funeral Customs and Rituals,» was actively utilized, where significant attention is given to memorial ritualism. The author extensively describes the dishes prepared for the memorial meal, discusses how they were prepared, and explores their significance. Rituals performed by relatives of the deceased on the day of the burial and throughout the annual memorial cycle are also detailed. Equally important for this study is Volodymyr Shukhevych's monograph, «Hutsulshchyna,» particularly the fourth volume dedicated to family ritualism. Regarding memorial customs, Volodymyr Shukhevych describes the mountain dwellers' rituals related to memorial motifs in the calendar. The work places considerable emphasis on memorial dishes and their sacred significance. Among the sources crucial for the study of funeral and memorial ritualism, I want to mention the following authors: H. Vovk, F. Kolessa, Z. Kuzel, A. Onyshchuk, I. Sventsitsky, I. Franko, Ya. Faltkovsky, and O. Kolberg.

Roman Huziy made a significant contribution to the study of funeral and memorial ritualism among Ukrainians. His work «Funeral Customs and Rituals» deserves attention, containing information about pre-funeral, funeral, and memorial customs and rituals of highlanders. It is noteworthy that the author separately highlights all the peculiarities of population groups present in the region of the Ukrainian Carpathians. He also compares the features of funeral ritualism among highlanders with the overall Ukrainian and Slavic traditions. This work spans the period from the early 19th century to the last decades of the 20th century. Additionally, other articles by Roman Huziy on funeral and memorial customs are worth mentioning.

In general, the funeral and memorial ritualism in Pokuttia was studied by authors such as L. Levynovska, A. Kilar, M. Pankiv, I. Koval-Fuchilo, I. Fitsak, I. Cherlenyak, O. Tsyhanyuk, M. Yaremchuk, L. Kostyuk, Ya. Samotis, and S. Ulyanovska.

When it comes to memorial motifs in the calendar, Cornelius Kutelmakh made a significant contribution. Among his works utilized for this research are two articles: «Polissya-Carpathian Parallels in the Overall Ukrainian Calendar-Ritual Sphere,» published in 1994, and «Ancient Basis in the Calendar Ritualism of Carpathian Ukrainians,» published in 1995. Both articles were published in the ethnographic journal «Narodoznavchi Zoshiti.» In these articles, the author draws parallels between the Carpathian and overall Ukrainian memorial calendar-ritual tradition.

Another important work related to funeral and memorial customs is the article by Zoryana Nebesna titled «Funeral Traditions of Ukrainians in Boykivshchyna at the End of the 20th – Beginning of the 21st Century,» published in 2009. In this article, the author provides information about pre-funeral, funeral, and memorial customs of the Boykos. This research is interesting because its chronological boundaries cover the late 20th to the early 21st century, documenting contemporary customs. This allows us not only to analyze the preservation of certain customs in the present but also to trace their evolution based on earlier research.

I would like to highlight Svitlana Boyan's work «Main Christian Holidays of the Calendar Ritual Complex of the Boykos,» published in 2008. In this work, the author thoroughly describes memorial customs and rituals of the inhabitants of Boykivshchyna for each of the major Christian holidays. Equally important for the research was Vasyl Ivanchuk's article «Individual and Calendar Memorial-Manistic Rituals in Hutsulshchyna,» published in 2021. The author describes memorial days throughout the year and characterizes the main features of memorial traditions in the calendar in Hutsulshchyna.

The primary source base for the study of funeral and memorial ritualism includes ethnographic literature, field materials, publications by domestic and foreign authors, archival and manuscript data.

CHAPTER 1. PRE-FUNERAL RITUALISM

1.1. Conceptions of Death

Customs that every family inevitably encounters are funeral and memorial rituals. At the same time, these are the most enduring and well-preserved rituals. It's worth noting that the funeral ritual has a specific impact on participants. It was perceived as a means to transport the deceased to the «other world» while simultaneously protecting the living from the detrimental influence of death. In the 20th century, people understand death as the end of everything, whereas archaic thinking perceived it in the context of an end-beginning cycle. That's why old rituals and customs are often incomprehensible to contemporary individuals.

Death has always been perceived by people as a great sorrow, and at the same time, they understood its inevitability: «If they didn't die, they would hold up the sky.» According to folk beliefs, a person had three substances: body, soul, and spirit. Death meant the separation of the soul and spirit from the body. However, while the soul left the body permanently, the spirit supposedly could return to the body, which was considered unnatural.

In various regions of Ukraine, including Pokuttia, there are customs and precautions observed by people when death is imminent. According to A. Onyshchuk's records in the village of Karliv in the Sniatyn region, there was a prohibition on sleeping when someone was dying in the house. The person who was sleeping at the moment of someone's passing was always awakened «so that they wouldn't sleep in peace,» as they might get frightened upon waking up. It was also believed that such a person might not wake up at all and could die. Similar warnings about sleeping at specific times during the ritual period are recorded both in Pokuttia and other regions of Ukraine. For example, in the Hordynia region, it was believed that when there was a deceased person in the village, no one should sleep during the day, «otherwise, there would be a curse on the household» (judgment).

The practice influenced by protective motives, noted by I. Voloshchynskyi in Pokuttya villages, is interesting. Before the father's death, the son would go around the entire household, as otherwise «bad things would happen, the household would decline, and there would be nothing joyful about it.»

The population of the Boykivshchyna region, based on religious affiliation, being Christians, associates their concepts of death more with the reunion of the entire family «on the other side» than with forgetting or the tragedy associated with the loss of a relative.

According to tradition, Jesus Christ, through His resurrection, granted eternal life after death, which needed to be earned through good deeds during earthly life. As for the Hutsul region's population, death was considered a natural outcome of life, a deserved result, an embodiment of universal justice. Many researchers acknowledge death as a natural consequence of life.

Among the Hutsuls, there are several types of death agonies; for example, a light death is quick, coming to a person suddenly so that they may not even feel it. However, this was considered only the «right» death: in old age, after reconciling with the world, settling all material matters. One had to live a virtuous life and, in return, receive death as liberation from all life burdens. «Adam died; it will be our turn.» Other types of death were seen as a violation of God's commandments. Such a death was «not one's own,» «unexpected,» sudden: it could seize a person on the road, lurk in the water or the forest, somewhere unexpectedly, unprepared for this crucial transition. Thus, the Hutsuls adhered to the widespread Ukrainian belief: «We go not when we want but when called.» This belief can be recognized as a common constant since it is not only known but actively used throughout Ukraine.

As everywhere in Ukraine, in Lemkivshchyna, death was considered a natural and inevitable end to earthly life, a universal law to which every person is subject, regardless of their material and social status. Folk sayings such as «No one can buy themselves out of death» and «Death chooses without distinction, be it a lord or Ivan» also attest to traditional notions of the universality of the law of death. Traditional beliefs about the universality of the law of death, as well as the conviction of the incorruptibility of the demonic character embodying it, found reflection in the folk legends and song creativity of the highlanders.

Therefore, we see that traditional beliefs about death in Pokuttia share common features with other historical and ethnographic regions of Ukraine. It was generally believed that a person consisted of three substances: body, soul, and spirit. Similarly, funeral and memorial rituals in Pokuttia, like those throughout Ukraine, are the most enduring and best-preserved. This is primarily explained by the fact that the funeral ritual had a specific impact on participants, as it was considered a means to transport the deceased to the «other world» while simultaneously protecting the living from the detrimental influence of death.

1.2. Death Prognostication

There are numerous traditional beliefs in the Pokuttia region associated with a person's death. Most often, people learn about someone's impending death through dreams. However, unusual behavior of domestic animals, birds, mysterious sounds inside or outside the house, falling or breaking of objects, and the dying person's own sensations also serve as indications. Families with a terminally ill member anticipate the approaching death and prepare for the event. If a seriously ill person dreams of a deceased person or if departed relatives come to communicate, it foretells imminent death. However, if the dreamer remains silent, it does not signify death.

Foretelling death was also practiced through:

- Dreams (seeing a priest, a wedding, losing a tooth, corn, falling into a pit, crossing a trench – indicating someone's death or the dreamer's childhood).

- The sick person's behavior (excessive sleep, staring at hands, talking about a journey).

- The behavior of specific birds and animals (a dog howling, a candle extinguishing for no reason, a swallow entering the house, a bird hitting the window, cries of an owl or nightjar near the house).

- The appearance of the deceased (open eyes, a fresh look in Verbyvtsi; if no one in the village died for six months after the funeral, the deceased would take someone from the family to the afterlife).

An ominous sign is when smoke from an extinguished candle on Christmas Eve goes towards the door, indicating that someone in the family will die that year. Bringing a deceased person from another settlement for burial is considered a bad omen, predicting many deaths in the village.

According to ancient beliefs, following the death of the head of the household, domestic animals or crops might perish, and there would be a decline in agricultural productivity. In the village of Karliv in the Sniatyn district, when the head of the household was dying, someone would quickly go to the granary and move the grain «that he still had in his hands so that it wouldn't freeze.» It was believed that failure to do so would result in poor crop yield. In other villages in Pokuttia, seeds are moved for the same purpose when carrying the deceased out of the yard, and livestock is untied.

Witnessing the critical condition of the sick, relatives would summon a priest for confession and communion. There were instances where family members could, with their cries, call a person back from the afterlife, thus prolonging their life for a few more days.

For example, in the Boykivshchyna region, during the pre-death period, if the dying person could, they would give instructions to the family regarding the funeral, specifying what to wear, how to mourn, divide property, land, household, and so on. Interesting succession traditions in Boykivshchyna were described by I. Franko, including the tradition of appointing a «trustee.» At that time, a dying person had to settle debts and reconcile with enemies. This practice persisted into the first decades of the 20th century. As a sign of forgiveness, people would shake hands, sometimes even kissing. Over time, it evolved into the dying person asking for forgiveness for sins, and the attendees saying, «May God forgive» three times. They would also invite a priest for confession and communion. If the dying person was in the hospital, the priest would be brought to the patient's room.

In the Hutsul region at the beginning of the 20th century, when Hutsuls were actively engaged in crafts such as weaving or sewing, they also observed craft-related processes. The length of the thread on the wedding wreath before the ceremony was considered an important and telling omen for the future: a long thread symbolized a long life, while a short one indicated a swift death.

In conclusion, it can be summarized that in Pokuttia, as well as universally in Ukraine, death omens included: parents' dreams (most commonly), unusual behavior of birds and domestic animals, the sick person's abnormal behavior or premonitions, sighing of trees, and so on.

1.3. Traditional Ways to Ease the Dying Process

Very often in the folk traditions, situations arise and have arisen where it is challenging for a person to release a sinful soul. In such cases, the relatives of the dying person performed specific actions to ease the transition into eternity. One way to facilitate the transition of the «soul» is through a «passionate» candle. This candle is given only to those who are seriously ill, to alleviate their suffering. The flame of the candle represents «the bright path that the soul wanders.» Believers believed that one should not cry for the deceased because the dying person would suffer greatly, and crying could frighten the «soul,» separating from the body and causing additional anguish in the dying person.

Additionally, to alleviate the agony, they would remove the pillow from under the person's head, as, according to beliefs, the feathers could scald the person's body and hinder the departure of the soul. Since ancient times among the Boykos, there existed the notion of a «light» or «heavy» death. So, when they saw that a person was suffering for a long time and could not die, they spread a rolled-up cloth under them and placed it crisscross across the entire house. The dying person was dressed in clean white clothes and the bed was remade. There is a tradition of moving the dying person onto a «dolivka» because, according to pre-Christian beliefs, the earth has purifying power, or it is a transition for the person to the afterlife.

It is also essential to mention the prolonged agony of witches and healers who could not die on their own. To alleviate their suffering, people would create a hole in the ceiling or sometimes dismantle the roof. This practice may be remnants of a pagan custom of carrying the deceased's body not through the door but through a special opening.

Various special measures aimed at easing the dying process were taken with the onset of agony, especially in cases of a difficult death. For instance, instead of a pillow under the person's head, a sacred herb or a cloth, in which the sanctified Easter bread was carried to the church, would be placed. Prolonged pre-mortem torments and a difficult death were considered by the people as God's punishment for a sinful life, with angels and demons struggling for the person's soul.

For comparison, in the Lemko region, to alleviate the physical and spiritual suffering of a dying person shortly before their apparent death, relatives would summon a priest to the home. The priest would provide confession, communion, and anoint the believer with consecrated oil. Additionally, a farewell gathering was arranged for the dying person to bid farewell to all family members, neighbors, friends, and even enemies. Responding to the dying person's call for forgiveness, those present would approach one by one, saying three times, «I forgive you, may the Lord God forgive you.» They believed that this collective absolution of the person's sins ensured a smooth transition of the soul to the world of ancestors. Even in the case of sudden death, everyone who had conflicts with the deceased would visit the mourning house and express a similar «farewell» formula.

They would also place a lit «thunderbolt» or crucifix in the person's hands and give them consecrated water. They would read akathists or special prayers «for the repose of the soul» and always refrain from excessive displays of grief to avoid diverting the soul from its chosen path. In the case of a difficult death of a child in some villages of Northern Lemko, they would cover the child with the mother's skirt or wedding scarf or ask the godparents to hold the child in their arms. The Boykos also had the practice of tearing the roof of the house to ease the agony in the case of a severe death.

To expedite the departure of the soul from the body, various magical items and talismans were used, such as candles, consecrated water, crucifixes, wedding attributes, and they refrained from crying and making noise (as they said in the Zhytomyr region, «crying will drive away the soul»), and more. Alongside these peculiar details (ritualized farewell to the dying, the practice of drilling a hole in the wall of the house, the protective use of poppy, candles from the first communion, Paschal linen), in general, it can be said that these and other customs of the highlanders have many analogies in the traditions of the entire Ukrainian population and, broadly, various European nations.

Therefore, we can summarize briefly that to alleviate the agony, the following actions were often performed: removing the pillow from under the head, placing a crucifix in the hands, sprinkling with holy water, transferring the dying person to a special spot, opening windows or doors, punching holes in the walls or ceiling (depending on the region), in the Boyko region, opening up the house, and so on. A common feature for almost all ethnographic regions was the prohibition of crying for the dying relatives to ease the soul's departure from the body.

Hence, funerals are always something unpleasant for people because we always lose our loved ones. It is important to understand that it is a completely natural process of ending human life, so whether we like it or not, we must come to terms with it. Even during life, a person can only imagine what will happen to them after earthly life. In different regions of Ukraine, beliefs vary, but it all comes down to the idea that for a person to have a good eternal life, they must live well on earth. People pay attention to various signs that can be harbingers of death. Most often, these are dreams or domestic animals, and birds also often signal the approach of death. There are cases when it is challenging to «release the sinful soul,» and folk traditions have always provided a series of measures to ease this process. Highlanders, being Christians by religious affiliation, partly explain the similarity of their traditions with those of the entire Ukrainian population. Still, in their funeral traditions, there are also pre-Christian rituals that resonate with the customs of many Slavic peoples.

CHAPTER 2. FUNERAL RITUALS

2.1. Preparation for the Funeral

One of the initial stages of preparing for a funeral was the announcement of the death. In the Pokuttia region, the open gates of the yard, which remained open from the time of death until the burial, and the church bells ringing intermittently three times, were used to notify people about someone's passing.

Similarly to other regions in Ukraine, the ways of announcing the death of fellow villagers and relatives varied in the Carpathians. The news of a death could be conveyed orally, using special sound signals, or through visual means. One distinctive mourning tradition was observed among the Hutsuls, where unique practices such as lighting a fire near the deceased's house, hanging a piece of cloth on the window, and playing the trembita were common. It's worth noting that the tradition of notifying with the trembita is still present among the Hutsuls and even in some villages on the border of the Boyko-Lemko region. Most of the mentioned customs and traditions have persisted to this day, as they were documented not long ago in this territory, specifically at the beginning of the 20th century.

In different areas of the Boykivshchyna and partly in the Hutsul region and Bukovyna, signaling functions were performed by wailing. In the Carpathians, a person wailed, known as «yoikala,» expressing the pain of an irreparable loss. This behavior was a way of not holding the grief within oneself. Funeral wailing often touched upon the virtues of the deceased and how challenging it would be for the family after the burial without their relative. This practice was part of the funeral ritual. It was crucial not to wail after sunset, during the night. In the Hutsul region, it was common to hire mourners known as «plachky.»

The custom of announcing a death through wailing was also practiced among some South Slavic peoples. The funeral customs of the Romanians included trumpet playing and lighting a fire. The tradition of notifying about death with church bells is more widely known among European nations.

Importantly, among Ukrainians in the Carpathians, especially among Boykos and Lemkos, there are specific customs and superstitions related to funeral tolling. Different tolling patterns are observed for deceased individuals of various ages and genders, with particular attention given to the superstitions surrounding tolling for suicides.

The next stage of funeral rituals is the preparation of the deceased's body. After death, the deceased is allowed to lie for at least two hours, after which the elders wash and dress them in pre-prepared clothes. The water used for washing is poured in a place where no one walks, such as at the base of an elderberry bush or where 2-3 crossroads or fences converge. K. Mrochek notes that in Zavally, such a place is called «sutytsya»; anyone who steps on it will die in severe and prolonged agony. Residents of Cheremkhovo believe that anyone stepping on a spot where such water was poured will experience leg pain and may even become crippled. The comb used to groom the deceased and the clothing they wore are burned. After this, the deceased is placed in one of the following ways:

- Directly into the coffin, on the catafalque – 8 (Troitsya, Nyzhniv, Repuzhynets, Rashkiv, Oliyevo-Korolivka, Potochysche, Vikno, Stryhantsi).

- In the coffin, on the table – 5 (Obertyn, Prykmyshche, Zhukiv, Dubky, Korshiv).

- On the catafalque – 11 (Ostrivets, Tyshkivtsi, Chekhova, Chernyatin, Verbyvtsi, Zhivachiv, Hlushkiv, Luka, Torhovytsia, Mala Kamyanka, P'yadyky).

The head of the deceased should be turned towards the icons, and the feet towards the door. A pillow stuffed with straw is placed under the head. The hands are crossed, and a candle is placed (Horodenkivshchyna). Men are dressed in a new suit. A four-fold folded kerchief is placed near the woman's head.

Unmarried boys and girls are dressed as if for a wedding, a wreath is made of periwinkle, cornflowers, or artificial flowers. Girls have their hair let down. A large wreath is placed around the body, and after the burial, it is hung on the grave cross. Unmarried men are also placed rings in the coffin.

In the early 20th century in the Boykivshchyna region, washing the deceased was mainly done by poor people who earned a living this way. Today, it is typically done by relatives and close people. If there are no close relatives, neighbors or caretakers take on this responsibility. Items such as the comb, mattress, straw, and clothing that had physical contact are burned. Women wash female bodies, while men wash male bodies. If a man died at a young age, he was dressed in an embroidered shirt, typically a wedding one. Nowadays, it is usually the attire the deceased wore during their lifetime, but if it is a woman, she is dressed in festive clothing that she liked during her life. There was an understanding of «death attire,» mainly for older and sick people. A distinctive practice was the burial of unmarried girls and boys, where older unmarried girls were traditionally buried in a wedding dress, with rings placed regardless of their engagement status. A small tree was made, adorned with artificial flowers, and placed near the cross after the burial. Nowadays, a large bouquet of white flowers is made and placed near the cross, along with special wreaths.

It is essential to mention the prohibition of dressing the deceased in the clothing of another living person, as it is believed that doing so may lead to the death of that person.

People were cautious about «dead» water, the water used for washing the deceased. This attitude was not exclusive to the Carpathian region but widespread throughout Ukraine. In the Hutsul region, it was referred to as «special water.» It was crucial to neutralize this water, often by pouring it immediately after washing. There was a widespread belief that «dead water» could be used for harm or misfortune, especially by those who had knowledge, often local healers and witches. It was always poured in places where no one walks, considering both people and domestic animals, and «where the sun does not shine.» This was likely a symbolic way of emphasizing the potential danger of this water, as its practical implementation was challenging. When a person passed through such water, they would fall ill or face misfortunes. Similar warnings applied to the towels used for washing the deceased, which were also burned. Symbolically, washing the body not only meant purification but also aimed at eliminating signs characteristic of a living person.

In general, these customs belong to the overall Ukrainian traditions and have many counterparts in the customs of Slavic and other European nations. Some distinctive details indicating differences in funeral practices among residents of various Carpathian regions include avoiding the use of a belt in funeral attire. It was also customary to equip the deceased with a bag, purse, and the practice of adorning handmade wax rings with gold plating. The tradition of dressing the deceased only in white clothes was maintained. It is important to mention some prohibitions, such as not touching the deceased with the hand used for sowing, not using well water for washing, pouring «dead» water into the river, and avoiding touching herbs or ash for cleansing purposes.

After preparing the deceased on the deathbed, all present washed their hands and sat down for the «first table.» On the table, a half-liter of vodka was placed, from which 100 grams were poured and placed on the windowsill. They also placed a glass or another container with wheat, into which a candle was inserted. The attendees prayed for the soul of the deceased, took a sip of vodka, had a bite to eat, prayed again, and then dispersed throughout the households.

During this time, they crafted a coffin for the deceased. Only after the deceased was dressed and placed on the catafalque did they start making the coffin and digging the grave. In recent decades, coffins and grave crosses are purchased from specialized ritual shops. Also, on the day of death, a grave is dug in the cemetery, with unmarried individuals and close relatives prohibited from digging the grave.

Therefore, funeral preparation is one of the most crucial and initial stages of funeral rites. When a person passes away, it is essential to inform relatives and close ones about the death. Various regions had different practices for this, but the overall Ukrainian tradition was mostly preserved. Immediately after death, preparations for the funeral begin, and many beliefs and precautions surround items that came into contact with the deceased. Once the deceased is ready, the making of the coffin and the digging of the grave commence.

2.2. Night Vigil by the Deceased's Body

When the deceased lies prepared on the catafalque, they are «surrounded by light» from all four sides: men by brothers, and women by sisters. All mirrors are covered with fabric so that death, the soul, does not «look» into them, and the deceased's reflection is not seen. On the first evening, a priest with a choir visits the deceased and performs a requiem service. On the second night, a deacon reads Psalms until midnight. From this time until the funeral, someone must always be near the deceased, mourning them. It was considered a sin to leave the deceased alone because «the body needs to be guarded.» Villagers also come to bid farewell, often bringing money in recent times. Upon entering the house with the deceased, visitors first recite the Lord's Prayer, then kiss the deceased's hand or cross, and only then greet others present. It is believed that «the dead, when lying in the coffin, sees and hears everything.» Therefore, arguing is not allowed in the house with the deceased because the body will be decomposing.

According to church canons, it is necessary to kiss only the cross lying near the deceased, not the deceased themselves, as it is just a body without a soul. Subsequently, the funeral is conducted for the soul, and prayers are offered specifically for the soul of the deceased, not for the body.

In the 19th to the early 20th century, games and other forms of ritualistic festivities existed. The original purpose of funeral festivities was evidently to protect the living and the deceased from evil forces, resist death, and magically affirm life in its various manifestations. Considering the well-known psychophysiological aspect of laughter as a means of relieving nervous tension and overcoming negative emotions, one can also highlight the positive psychotherapeutic effect of such actions for the participants in the ritual. The most widespread games in the Pokuttia region were «lubok,» «shybentsia,» «lords and servants,» and «work.» However, games at the deceased's place are no longer preserved. Instead, on the first night after the funeral, men may play cards, or engage in activities like tying someone to a table (Vikno, Potochysche, Oliievo-Korolivka), which is called «lubok.»

Several superstitions are associated with being in the deceased's house:

- If the deceased's right eye is half-open, it foretells that someone in the family will die, while if the left eye is half-open, it indicates a death in distant relatives.

- If the smoke from extinguished candles at the deceased's side goes towards the door, no one in the family will die. If it returns to the deceased, it is predicted that death will come for someone else.

- It is not acceptable to sweep the room where the deceased lies to prevent another family member from dying.

- Garbage is lifted under the «bench» (where the deceased lies), and when the body is taken out, it is immediately discarded to prevent the soul of the deceased from lingering or burned along with the remnants of household items.

The mourning of a deceased person has always been considered a sign of a «good» funeral. Many villagers believed that by wailing, they could wash away the sins of the deceased and ease their transition to the «other world.» Traditionally, women from the family, as well as godmothers and neighbors, were the main mourners. According to a customary requirement prevalent in villages even in the early 20th century, every village woman should be a good mourner. Inability to «initiate mourning» was as shameful as not knowing how to spin, weave, or work in the fields.

Interestingly, in some villages of Eastern Boykivshchyna, there was a tradition of hiring professional mourners for funerals, lasting until at least the 1940s. «To demonstrate how much the deceased's family regrets their loss, they mourned. This ritual was performed exclusively by relatives or hired a special choir of mourners. Sometimes the mourning could be heard almost throughout the entire village, especially if professional mourners were hired.»

The best-regarded were the lengthy poetic mourning chants, with poetic addresses and tender comparisons filled with sorrow. In the folk tradition, chanting by the deceased was called «zavodyty,» less frequently - «mourning the dead.» «Once we used to chant without fail. Daughters used to do it. Now, they still chant a bit, but not as much. They cry more.»

Example of a poetic mourning chant:

Oh, my master, my master,

It's not yet time for you to die,

You still had to manage,

Not to be taken away from us,

What a fine sunny day.

What a great day,

So, I will talk to you now,

Speak to us at least a word,

Because without you, it will be sad,

Because without you, it will be bitter.

You also knew the mistress,

And you arranged everything,

Added so much hard work,

And left your house,

But the other one – you bury underground,

There's not even a window,

And no light at all,

And it's so cold there,

And it's so heavy,

Oh, oh, oh.

An interesting phenomenon in Boyko mourning chants is the so-called «yoykannya,» where women loudly and prolongedly repeat «Oy-oy-oy!» Often, men also performed mourning chants, but only when a man lost his wife or child. Once, there was also a practice of priests chanting, but at the end of the 17th century, the bishop prohibited this custom because, in such a case, it seemed that Jesus Christ died in vain and rose again if church ministers mourn the deceased so fervently.

There were certain rules for performing mourning chants: they were chanted most loudly when visiting the deceased, when carrying out the household items, and near the grave. It was forbidden to cry over the coffin after sunset, and it was advised not to cry after the burial to avoid summoning the deceased and disturbing their peace. It was also forbidden for mothers to cry for their children. Folk sayings emphasized that when a child dies and the mother says goodbye, no tear should fall on the child because the child is an angel, and it is not good when tears are shed over them.

In conclusion, night vigils by the deceased's body are one of the most important rituals in the funeral cycle. It's also crucial to mention the ritual games near the deceased, which were prevalent not only among the Pokutians but also among the Boykos, Lemkos, and Hutsuls. However, this was documented at the end of the 19th to the beginning of the 20th century. Such customs were not recorded in the early 21st century. Additionally, funeral lamentations, which have been and continue to be an integral element of funeral rituals throughout Ukraine, should not be overlooked.

2.3. Funeral Rite

The next stage of the funeral ceremony was the burial ritual itself. The deceased, as the saying goes, «had to spend two nights in the house.» On the third day, they were buried, sometimes sooner, depending on natural conditions. Usually, the funeral begins before noon, occasionally after noon (Chekhova, Korshiv, Obertyn, Torhovyttsia) with the arrival of the priest accompanied by the church choir. Sometimes, especially if a young person has passed away, the funeral takes place with a brass band. However, it's worth noting that funerals with a brass band, encouraged by the Soviet authorities as a «new burial ritual without a priest,» hardly took root in the villages of Pokuttia. Depending on the person's social status, the funeral ceremony has its peculiarities. People who died during Holy Week were considered fortunate, as it was believed that their souls immediately went to heaven.

It is strictly forbidden to bury suicides with church honors. Earlier, their bodies were not even brought into the house from the scene of the tragedy; they were immediately taken to the cemetery, where a ready-made coffin awaited. On the same day, the body was buried on the edge of the cemetery. Often, even a cross was not installed. Now, in such cases, burials follow the usual script, except for actions related to the church and the priest. The priest, during the prayers for the deceased, also does not mention the name of the suicide, except in one prayer that includes the words: «...and those who, through darkness of mind, took their own lives...» But this happens extremely rarely. Suicides are buried on the outskirts of the cemetery. It is also forbidden to bury the unbaptized.

In folk beliefs, winds and storms are associated everywhere with evil demons and the souls of the deceased and suicides—drowners and hangers. Therefore, when the winds tear the roofs, people say, «Someone has hanged themselves.»

After the service in the house, the deceased is carried to the porch and taken outside. Personal belongings of the deceased, such as a watch, glasses, comb, hat, or scarf if they used one during their lifetime, are placed in the house. In Horodentsi, women pin a needle with thread in the folds. For a child, toys and sweets are placed (Cheremkhiv). The custom of placing necessary items for life into the coffin indicates that in the traditional spiritual culture of Ukrainians, as in many cultures worldwide, there was a steadfast belief that a person's death is only their transition from one world to another. Therefore, in the funeral rite, we find many elements aimed at ensuring certain conditions for the deceased's existence in the afterlife.

Only men who have already married off their children should carry the porch. The body is carried feet first, striking each threshold three times. During this time, relatives sit on the catafalque to ensure that no one in the family dies soon (Nezvysko, Yaseniv Pilnyi, Vikno), or everyone falls to the ground (Torhovyttsia).

After the body is carried out, where the deceased lay, they sprinkle the place with holy water and place some iron object (usually an axe) with bread on it (Nezvysko). They also open windows and doors for the soul to exit; otherwise, it would stay there and haunt until someone else dies in that house again (Zaluchchia). In the village of Vikno, they hold the bread on their knees, while, on the contrary, they close the windows and doors.

People waiting in the yard for the body to be carried out did not exchange verbal greetings or shake hands. If there was any conversation among them, it mostly revolved around the noble qualities of the deceased, without emphasizing any negative aspects. In this context, men would always remove their headgear, following an ancient custom. The funeral ceremony near the yard gathers all interested individuals without any invitation. The elders come to pay their respects, such as relatives, neighbors, and elderly people, while the young are mainly composed of most fellow villagers, especially the unmarried. During the funerals of unmarried individuals, separate elements of wedding rituals were performed, and in laments, as well as in poetic lyrics, the grave was compared to a bride or groom.

In the yard, the priest continues the service along with the choir, reciting the «proshcha» – the most important biographical milestones of the deceased's life. Also, near the deceased's house, relatives, friends, and neighbors bid farewell. At the end, the choir performs the deceased's farewell song. Upon leaving the yard, it is mandatory to take all the candles that were lit, as well as all the wreaths.

A significant part of the funeral ceremony is dedicated to laments. People lamented to avoid keeping all the grief and pain to themselves; it was as if they were sharing their sorrow with others, eliciting sympathy and understanding of their difficult situation. Funeral laments predominantly narrate the qualities of the deceased, the hardships awaiting the family, and their own sense of unhappiness.

The time when lamentations can begin and when they must end is always strictly defined. When the deceased's body is already laid on the funeral table or table, lamentations, with short breaks, continue constantly until the deceased is buried. Lamentations are not performed only at night, after sunset. During this time, the main task is to guard the soul of the deceased. Several main cycles of lamentations can be identified, each corresponding to a new stage of the funeral ritual: the arrival of people to the house to bid farewell to the deceased; the transfer of the body to the grave; carrying the body from the house, from the yard, the journey to the cemetery; lowering the funeral table. In some places, even in the XIX century, professional mourners were hired or invited. Nowadays, the prose texts of laments are partially improvised.

After the farewell in the yard, the deceased is transported to the church on special carriers:

- Carried by 13 villages (Vikno, Verbyvtsi, Cherniatyn, Dubky, Hlushkiv, Repuzhynets, Nyzhniv, Ostrivets, Chekhova, Olievo-Korolivka, Rashkiv, Potochysche, Stryhantsi), which is considered highly honorable.

- Transported by 11 villages (Torgovitsia, Korshiv, Mala Kamianka, Piadiky, Luka, Tyshkivtsi, Prykmishche, Obertyn, Zhyvachiv, Zhukiv, Troitsia).

During this time, the coffin can be:

- Open – 8 villages (Chekhova, Torgovitsia, Olievo-Korolivka, Potochysche, Ostrivets, Repuzhynets, Prykmishche, Zhyvachiv).

- Open outside and closed in the church – 8 villages (Korshiv, Piadiky, Vikno, Dubky, Tyshkivtsi, Verbyvtsi, Rashkiv, Obertyn).

- Closed – 8 villages (Hlushkiv, Cherniatyn, Luka, Troitsia, Zhukiv, Mala Kamianka, Stryhantsi, Nyzhniv).

From the yard, the funeral procession is arranged in the following order: ahead are some of the older men carrying the cross, followed by banners, then a portrait, after which women and children in pairs carry wreaths. Following them is the church choir or a brass band, then the priest and deacon, and four people carry the corners of the coffin lid (if the deceased is a man, men carry the lid, and if a woman, women carry it), followed by the coffin with the body. Relatives, close ones, and everyone who came to the funeral walk behind. Everyone carrying something has their right hand tied with a scarf, and small handkerchiefs are attached to the wreaths. Most participants carry candles, «so that the deceased can see the way to the other world» (Verbyvtsi, Chernelytsia).

On the way to the church, the funeral procession stops near chapels, crosses, at intersections, where the deceased most frequently walked. If a car approaches the funeral procession, it means there will be a new funeral in the village soon (Vikno). Even if an unfamiliar person meets the procession, they step aside and wait until it passes (men usually took off their headgear during this time). This also applied to vehicles: overtaking or bypassing a funeral procession is considered unacceptable.

The deceased is carried into the church, where the requiem service is held. The funeral table is placed in the middle of the church with the head towards the altar. If a priest passed away, the night before the funeral, the funeral table with the body was brought into the church, and it stayed there all night until the time of the requiem service by three priests from neighboring parishes and the procession to the cemetery.

In the church, during the priest's service, all crying and lamentations cease. Also, in the church, everyone present bids farewell to the deceased – the last kiss. It is believed that whoever kisses the cross last – a man or a woman of the same gender – will be next. At the cemetery, relatives bid farewell to the deceased once again. After this, the deceased is lowered into the grave on special belts. After sealing the grave, the priest sprinkles the pit and the funeral table with holy water. Before covering the pit, relatives throw a handful of soil after the priest, and after them, everyone else does the same. Children or grandchildren of the deceased have to «weave into the braid.»

Therefore, the funeral rite is the centerpiece of funeral and commemorative rituals, accompanied by numerous ritual prohibitions and observances. The ritual commenced in the home, continued in the yard, then the funeral procession moved to the church, where the ceremony continued, concluding at the cemetery when the priest sealed the grave and the coffin was buried. It is essential to emphasize that the funeral rite in Pokuttia has a nationwide character.

So, when a person passes away, their relatives begin preparations for the funeral. One of the initial stages is the announcement of this sad news, often communicated orally, such as ringing the church bell or trumpeting in the Hutsul region. Additionally, across Ukraine, lamentations served as a signaling function. The next stage involves washing and dressing the deceased's body. This stage is accompanied by numerous superstitions, mostly related to items that touched the deceased's body, as they were considered fatal. Special attention should be paid to the attitude towards water used to wash the bodies of the deceased. Only after washing the body and placing it on a catafalque did the crafting of the coffin and digging the grave begin.

In many villages, no money was taken for the coffin, as they understood that sooner or later, a similar situation might occur in their own family. However, in the 21st century, coffins are purchased from ritual service stores. The last stage before the funeral can be considered the night when the deceased stays in their own home. The deceased should not be left alone, with witnesses constantly present to guard against theft or the influence of evil forces. In the early 20th century, games were sometimes played near the deceased, aiming to bring some joy to the relatives.

CHAPTER 3. MEMORIAL RITUALS

3.1. Memorial Customs After Burial

After the funeral rites, memorial meals follow, which are common everywhere except in Obertin, where the priest canceled them. From the cemetery, all funeral attendees are invited to a communal prayer or «a meal.» Those who wish to pray and remember the deceased attend the meal, including the deacon with the church choir. Unmarried individuals, except for those who carried the deceased, are not allowed to attend the memorial meal. This prohibition likely serves to protect young people from death.

The feast begins with a prayer for the soul of the deceased and the serving of «kutia» (a type of porridge made from various grains grown in the local fields. Modern kutia is boiled wheat seasoned with honey). According to folk beliefs, each person present must taste kutia three times before the meal because «those who eat a few grains will only lift sins from the deceased.» In some places (villages of Pidvysotska, Mykulynets, Djuriv, Rusiv in Sniatyn district, Horodnytsia, Serafintsy, Rosokhach in Horodenka district, Zhabokruky, Bortnyky in Tlumach district), kutia was tasted only once, explaining that «for the heavenly kingdom of the deceased,» kutia «will lift sins from the soul.» A characteristic feature of this custom in other ethnographic regions of Ukraine and among Slavs in general is its association with cathartic magic – honey purifies, freeing a person from sins.

Honey was also consumed in memorial rituals. In Pokuttia, kutia with honey was prepared for nine, forty days («parastas to the church»), and on the anniversary of death. When someone died in a household with a beehive, honey was given for the soul of the deceased («service for the dead on watering Monday» in Rusiv village).

During the «meal,» a variety of food is served in large quantities, but it is not allowed to request any dish again. When serving cabbage, they pray again (Vikno).

At the end of the memorial meal, a collective prayer takes place, and the choir sings «Eternal Memory.» After this, only close relatives and neighbors remain in the deceased's house for the first night after the funeral. It is believed that the soul of the deceased is still in the house and can appear or give a sign, such as an insect (Vikno). The widespread belief that the soul continues its existence after death or unequivocally becomes a bird or some winged creature is prevalent among various peoples around the world.

On the second day, close relatives and neighbors are again summoned to go to the cemetery, where they light candles and pray at the grave. In the village of Nezvisko, they bring vodka and pieces of kalach, which they consume at the cemetery. In the village of Vikno, they also take a piece of sausage and leave it on the grave. Upon returning home, they remove curtains from windows and mirrors, distribute the vodka that stood on the windowsill among everyone, and give personal belongings of the deceased to relatives and neighbors. Sometimes the tradition of «gifts through the tree» on the day of the funeral has been preserved (Zabolotiv).

There is a belief that the deceased can take fellow villagers and relatives with them. In the time between the death of one person in the village and the death of another, it is said that the deceased is «on duty.» Often, the relatives of the deceased come to the funeral of a person taken by the deceased.

Mourning is an ancient and inseparable component of funeral rites – the expression of sorrow for the death of a person. Its origin is related to the ritualization of affective manifestations of grief and archaic ideas about the ritual expediency and moral-ethical significance of acts of public despair by the relatives and loved ones of the deceased. As a sign of mourning, relatives tie black ribbons on the gate or doors – 4 (Vikno, Tyshkivtsi, Ostivets, Chekhova).

Memorial services took place:

- after 9, 40 days, and a year, with an invitation to the deceased's house (Chekhova, Torgovitsia, Korshev, Verbivtsi, Luka, Dubki, Tyshkivtsi, Cherniatyn, Zhukiv, Obertin);

- invite only on the 40th day and after one year (Ostivets, Repuzhynets, Vikno, Hlushkiv, Olievo-Korolivka, Potochyshche, Rashkiv, Prykmishche, Zhivachiv, Nyzhniv, Troitsia, P'yadyky, Mala Kamyanka, Stryhantsi).

At the end of the meal, each guest is given a small loaf «for the repose of the soul.» Prayers for the souls of the deceased are also said on commemorative or memorial Saturdays – the last Saturday before November 8th, the feast of St. Demetrius. Relatives and neighbors are given special bread – panashok, and various sweets. Every year on major holidays – Easter (Vikno), Green holidays (Cherniatyn) – ceremonies take place at the graves.

After the funeral, relatives mourn the deceased family member. The mourning period varies according to the degree of family relationship. For parents, mother, child, brother, and sister, mourning lasts for a whole year, for grandparents – six or three months, and for more distant relatives – 40 days. During the mourning period, relatives are prohibited from singing, dancing, getting married, receiving guests, or going visiting. Men may also refrain from shaving for an extended period. Women wear black scarves for a year, believing that the soul still lingers with the family and requires assistance from the living. This assistance comes in the form of constant prayers for the soul of the deceased and reminiscences of their good deeds. On festive occasions and Sundays, candles are lit for the deceased, and occasionally, the priest is asked to pray for the souls of the relatives. Another unique custom is the «redemption» from mourning. After the mourning period, relatives, when going to dance for the first time, would throw a handful of coins under their feet. This act symbolized their redemption from the deceased (Verbyvtsi, Vikno).

Post-funeral customs also include the arrangement of cemeteries. Vinca, lovage, and mint are planted on graves, while fruit trees are planted near the head. The fruits from these trees are allowed for everyone to consume. However, selling these fruits is prohibited due to the belief that traded money will only bring financial losses. The decoration of graves in Pokuttia was considered a prestige for the living relatives. Therefore, Pokuttian rural cemeteries are always well-maintained, with many tombstones being artistic creations.

Immediately after the funeral ceremony, relatives of the deceased invited everyone to a memorial meal. Memorial services took place on the 9th day, 40 days, and the anniversary of the death. Closest relatives, neighbors, and those who helped with the funeral (preparing the body, making the coffin, and digging the grave) were invited. The relatives of the deceased observed mourning for some time after the funeral, usually expressed in clothing worn by relatives and household taboos.

3.2. Memorial Motifs in the Calendar

No season of the year, no cycle in the Ukrainian holiday calendar, and more specifically, no important date in the folk or church calendar can be imagined without honoring or at least remembering deceased loved ones. Perhaps that is why burial motifs, the actual rituals associated with commemorating deceased ancestors, have been quite well-preserved in both the calendar and domestic rituals.

This incredibly significant milestone in life was not to be forgotten, as in Ukrainian beliefs, the cult of ancestors was closely tied to the fertility cult. This connection is particularly evident in the reverence for ancestors influencing the fertility of the land, abundant harvests, and the prosperity of the family. The cemetery, a permanent residence for the deceased, became the main ceremonial site during this time. Here, besides various religious rituals, folk customs were performed, the semantics of which can be traced back to ancient times.

The term «commemoration of the deceased» is very close to the term «ancestor worship.» This is not accidental, as, according to researchers, commemorating the souls of the deceased is a later-transformed form of the archaic worship of ancestors (originally related only to the earliest ancestors). Therefore, we have every reason to use the term «ancestor worship» in this study in addition to the term «commemoration of the deceased.»

One of the central elements of the memorial ritual is the religious service. In general, religious services play a leading role in commemorating the deceased because prayer is the only thing they need from the living. When we hear someone's stories about dreams of deceased relatives or acquaintances, the usual plot is the deceased's request for a drink, food, medicine, or warm clothing. All these requests boil down to one thing – a request for prayer. In this way, people, whom daily concerns cause their relatives to forget, ask to be remembered in prayer, and the cost of a memorial or fence reflects the ambitions not of the one in eternity but of the living, who sometimes mistakenly believe that the more expensive the gravestone, the more sincere their love.

The commemoration ritual, regardless of the timing, followed a single scheme and included such obligatory stages: memorial church service, charity distribution, memorial dinner, and cemetery visits.

Memorial events begin with an evening meal on the eve of the canonical memorial date. Typically, in the afternoon, candles are lit in the house, a lamp in front of the icons, and the reading of the Psalter begins. Coming to remember the deceased is the duty of all who interacted with them. In the house, they prepare dishes similar to those served at the funeral.

In addition to commemorating individual deceased persons, there are memorial days when all the departed are honored. These are universal memorial Saturdays. On these days, souls are remembered in the church. Bread is brought to the church for this purpose, and at home, families cook porridge, borscht, soup, mushrooms, fish, bake fresh bread, and remember together. On the evening before Christmas, every family gathers around the table and commemorates. The names of fasts (Philip's, Meatfare, Great, Peter's, etc.) are names of memorial Saturdays for all the deceased, whom, according to villagers, should be «remembered for their peace» on these days. Therefore, on such Saturdays, bread is brought to the church, which is then used for the evening commemoration at home.

Throughout Ukraine, Orthodox memorial services are established in the liturgical calendar. These include five universal memorial Saturdays: Meatfare, Trinity, and the 2nd, 3rd, and 4th Saturdays of Great Lent. Established memorial days include Monday of Butter Week, which is the second Monday or Sunday after Easter (farewells, «mohylky»), September 11 – the Beheading of St. John the Baptist, and Dmitry's Saturday. On memorial days, relatives of the deceased go to the church, then to the cemetery. Where the memorial service took place, a feast begins. This tradition, collective commemorations, or public memorial services, persists to this day. Ancient rituals of laying not only dishes and delicacies but also flowers and candles on the grave are still observed.

On farewells, relatives place Easter eggs and sweets on the graves of their loved ones, collected by children. When they go to the cemetery, they paint eggs (Easter eggs are not placed on the graves), take a piece of bread, and put everything in a scarf or towel, laying it on the grave. On Easter, a general commemoration of all the deceased takes place, and the priest walks through the cemeteries. Those who wish can order a memorial service «Za khodzhenniam» – walking around the cemetery, singing and thus performing the memorial service, and those who order individually receive a short «Lity.»

The observance of mourning by relatives is associated with the annual memorial cycle or at least certain dates. Throughout the 19th and early 20th centuries, the main manifestations of the annual memorial cycle included specific features of the daily clothing of family members, restrictions on certain household activities, participation in entertainment, and festive events. The observance of these guidelines by Lemkos still holds significant ritual and ethical importance. They condemn any manifestation of disrespect for the memory of the deceased. In the early years, they visited their graves, especially on major holidays, sometimes bringing remnants of food or sweets to the grave. However, unlike neighboring ethnic groups, Lemkos did not pay much attention to the graves of their ancestors. When wooden crosses decayed on them, the graves overgrew with grass and were forgotten. Only occasionally did they plant favorite trees of the deceased on the graves, leaving a memory of them.

After the funeral, relatives of the deceased must wear mourning for them. It is worth noting that the concept of mourning often reduces to the appropriate color of clothing, accessories, and a prohibition on using bright colors. Until the mid-20th century, Lemkos wore clothing of white color, unlike other ethnic groups who wore black mourning attire.

Traditionally, mourning is worn for one to two years for parents, and for grandparents, it can extend to three to four months. Parents mourning for their children often do not abandon grief for many years or even throughout their entire lives. Manifestations of mourning include adherence to certain fasting periods, especially before the Feast of Saints Peter and Paul. Parents who have lost children are forbidden to eat fruits until the Transfiguration, so that the child is not deprived of them in the afterlife. Mourning is not observed for unbaptized young children because they are considered pure angels who do not require any atonement. Mourning for suicides should include constant repentance in prayers and charitable acts on their behalf to atone for their sins. Saint John Chrysostom speaks about it as follows: «Let us try, as much as possible, to help the departed not with tears, not with mourning, not with expensive tombs, but with our prayers and offerings, so that in this way, they may receive the promised blessings.»

For the commemoration of «unclean» deceased individuals, there are also special days, not of the church but of the folk calendar. This primarily includes the Navsky Easter or Rusalka Easter, which falls on the Thursday before Trinity. On this day, suicides, drownings, and deceased unbaptized children are remembered. The described customs and superstitions relate to natural death. If a person ended their life by suicide, they were buried without a priest, bells, or funeral ritual at the suicide location, on the border between two plots, or beyond the cemetery fence. Anyone passing by a suicide site would throw a stone at it, resulting in the formation of tall graves. Now suicides are also buried in the Cemeteries of the Homeless, Beggars, and Travelers, a community cemetery.

Therefore, practically every major Christian holiday among the highlanders was accompanied by ritual actions that, to a greater or lesser extent, involved funeral, agrarian, zoomorphic, and marital motifs. The basis of rituals, customs, and traditions during Christian holidays in Pokuttia is quite stable, despite the local variability of individual elements. It can be said that funeral motifs are vividly expressed in the winter, spring, summer, and autumn calendar-folk rituals. Such rituals have quite archaic origins, especially in the rituals related to fire and ritual feasts, which were direct communication with the souls of the deceased. Of course, ancient customs have come down to us in rudimentary form, but their significance has not lost its power. All these actions reflect spiritual contact with ancestors, thanks to which the souls of the deceased loved ones are responsible for the well-being of the family and a good harvest. This testifies that traditions have not been forgotten over the millennia but still hold a prominent place in the life of the Ukrainian people.

CONCLUSIONS

Therefore, based on the research results, the following conclusions can be drawn:

1. In conclusion, it can be noted that the main goal of the study was achieved – identifying the historical and ethnographic features of funeral and commemorative rituals among the inhabitants of Pokuttia in the second half of the 19th to the first half of the 20th century. To achieve this goal, a significant amount of work was carried out, involving the analysis of a considerable amount of specialized literature and sources. These books and articles mainly focused on funeral, burial, and commemorative rituals, and also included works dedicated to neighboring historical and ethnographic regions, aiming at conducting a comparative analysis of ritual complexes and identifying common and distinctive features. The most common features were observed in the rituals of Hutsul, Boyko, and Lemko regions.

2. Funeral and commemorative rituals in Pokuttia in the 20th and 21st centuries constitute a vast complex of customs and rituals that encompass ancient and modern cultural phenomena, combining various characteristics of folk customs and Christian cultural rituals. An important feature is the preservation of rare archaisms over a

considerable period. Analyzing a significant body of literature allows us to conclude that many phenomena present today are remnants of customs and rituals with roots tracing back to ancient Slavic times. Importantly, all these practices found their continuation during the era of Kyivan Rus and subsequent periods.

3. Funeral traditions in each region and for each ethnographic group have their own local specificity, meaning that each area has its own customs and rituals passed down from generation to generation. When considering funeral rituals in the context of all Ukraine, we see that they are based on a folk worldview that originated from many pre-Christian rituals and cults influenced by the Christian church. A characteristic feature of funeral customs among the population of the Ukrainian Carpathians is their long-lasting stability and resistance to ritual innovations. Therefore, while having a nationwide basis, funeral customs in the Carpathians still stand out with certain local peculiarities resulting from the region's unique historical, political, economic, and cultural-ethnic development.

4. Many ancient traditions among Ukrainians, including those in the Carpathian region, are associated with commemorating the deceased and, in general, honoring the memory of ancestors. This includes the custom of arranging memorial feasts on specific days in honor of the deceased (known as individual commemorations);

various forms of ritual «feeding» of the deceased (leaving sacrificial food in the house, church, or cemetery and gifting it to the poor on annual and calendar commemorations); and a well-known practice in various regions of Ukraine, including the Carpathians (mainly in Hutsulshchyna), of consuming ritual porridge with honey known as «kolyvo,» «kutia,» or «pshenytsia» during commemorations.

5. Funeral and commemorative motives in the calendar of each region and for each ethnographic group have their own local peculiarities, meaning that each region has its own customs and rituals passed down from generation to generation. When considering funeral and commemorative rituals in the context of all Ukraine, we see that they are rooted in a folk worldview formed based on many pre-Christian rituals and cults influenced by the Christian church. A characteristic feature of commemorative customs among the population of the Ukrainian Carpathians is their long-lasting stability and resistance to ritual innovations. Therefore, while having a nationwide basis, they still stand out with certain local peculiarities, arising from the uniqueness of the region's historical, political, economic, and cultural-ethnic development.

6. Despite some differences, the foundation of commemorative rituals is common for residents of various localities in the Carpathians and Ukraine as a whole, as well as for many European nations. This

kinship can be explained by interregional and interethnic historical-cultural connections and influences, as well as the similarity of pre-Christian beliefs and Christian customs, and the uniformity of the church commemorative ritual. A significant feature of funeral and commemorative customs among Ukrainian highlanders is their long-standing and unchanging attitude against ritual innovations. Despite socio-cultural influences in modern times, some customs, such as mourning, protective-purifying, sacrificial, and commemorative elements of the traditional ritual in contemporary funerals of Pokuttia, have retained their local characteristics to this day.

LIST OF USED SOURCES AND LITERATURE

I. Sources

1. Vovk, Khvedir. «Ethnographic Features of the Ukrainian People.» Studies in Ukrainian Ethnography and Anthropology. Kyiv: Mystetstvo, 1995. 335.

2. Hnatiuk, Volodymyr. «Funeral Customs and Rituals.» Ethnographic Collection. Vol. 31-32, Lviv: Shevchenko Scientific Society, 1912. 131-424.

3. Kolberg, Oskar. Tales of Pokuttya. Uzhhorod: Karpaty, 1991. 327.

4. Kuzelia, Zenon. «Feasts and Entertainments during the Wake in the Ukrainian Funeral Ritual.» Ethnographic Collection. Vol. 121, Lviv: Shevchenko Scientific Society, 1914. 173-224.

5. Kuzelia, Zenon. «Ukrainian Funeral Customs and Rituals in Ethnographic Literature.» Ethnographic Collection. Vol. 31-32, Lviv: Shevchenko Scientific Society, 1912. 133-202.

6. Onyshchuk, Antin. «Funeral Customs and Rituals in the Village of Zelenytsia, Nadvirna District.» Ethnographic Collection. Vol. 31-32, Lviv: Shevchenko Scientific Society, 1912. 231-252.

7. Sventsitskyi, Iarion. «Funeral Laments.» Ethnographic Collection. Lviv: Shevchenko Scientific Society, 1912. 1-129.

8. Filaret, Kolessa. «Beliefs about the Soul and Afterlife in Ukrainian Funeral and Memorial Rituals.» Ethnographic Collection. Vol. 242, Lviv: Shevchenko Scientific Society, 2001. 7-82.

9. Franko, Ivan. «Galician-Ruthenian Folk Proverbs.» Ethnographic Collection. Vol. 2, Lviv: Shevchenko Scientific Society, 1907. 300.

10. Shukhevych, Volodymyr. «Hutsul Region.» Ethnographic Collection. Vol. 4, Lviv: Shevchenko Scientific Society, 1904. 271.

11. Falkowski, Jan. Northeastern Borderlands of Hutsulshchyna. Lviv: Towarzystwo Ludoznawcze, 1938. 105.

12. Kolberg, Oskar. «Pokucie,» Ethnographic Image. Vol. 1. Krakow: Jagiellonian University Press, 1882. 367.

II. Literature

1. Artyukh, Lida. «Memorial Dishes in Polissia (Folk Etiquette).» Polissia of Ukraine: Materials of Historical and Ethnographic Research. Lviv: Institute of Folklore NAS of Ukraine, 1997. 316.

2. Boyan, Svitlana. «Major Christian Holidays of the Calendar Ritual Complex of the Boykos.» Ukraine: Cultural Heritage, National Consciousness, Statehood 17 (2008): 492-500.

3. Vasylechko, Leonid. Paths of Echoes. Ivano-Frankivsk: Nova Zoria, 2003. 286.

4. Voytovych, Nadiya. Folk Demonology of the Boykivshchyna. Lviv: Spolom, 2015. 237.

5. Halaychuk, Volodymyr. «From the Spiritual Culture of Bohorodchany: Customs, Beliefs, and Beliefs Related to Worldview Ideas about Death and the Deceased.» Mythology and Folklore 3-4 (2010): 27-49.

6. Hlushko, Mykhailo. Methodology of Field Ethnographic Research: A Textbook. Lviv: Ivan Franko National University, 2008. 288.

7. Hrymich, Marina. «Old Age. Death. Culture of Honoring the Deceased.» Folk Culture of Ukrainians: Life Cycle of a Human. Vol. 5, Kyiv: Dulibi, 2015. 432.

8. Huziy, Roman. «Funeral Customs and Rituals.» Ethnogenesis and Ethnic History of the Population of the Ukrainian Carpathians. Vol. 2. Lviv: Institute of Folklore NAS of Ukraine, 2006. 589.

9. Huziy, Roman. «Zenon Kuzelia – Researcher of Funeral Rituals of Ukrainians.» Ethnographic Notebooks 6 (2000): 1012-1016.

10. Huziy, Roman. «Folk Means of Facilitating the Process of Mourning.» Ethnographic Notebooks 3 (1998): 330-334.

11. Huziy, Roman. «Protective Customs and Warnings Related to Approaching Death: Comparative Studies.» Carpathians: Man, Ethnos, Civilization: Scientific Journal on the Problem of Carpathian Studies 1 (2009): 163-168.

12. Huziy, Roman. «Ritual Mourning of the Deceased in the Funeral Customs of the Carpathian Ukrainians.» Ethnographic Notebooks 6 (2000): 809-815.

13. Huziy, Roman. «Traditional Ways of Escorting the Deceased to the Cemetery in the Funeral Customs of the Carpathian Ukrainians.» Ethnographic Notebooks 3 (2001): 528-531.

14. Huziy, Roman. «Traditional Ways of Announcing Death in the Funeral Customs of the Carpathian Ukrainians.» Ethnographic Notebooks 5 (1998): 693-696.

15. Huziy, Roman. «Perceptions and Beliefs of Carpathian Ukrainians about Personified Death.» Ethnographic Notebooks 6 (1995): 362-366.

16. Ivanchuk, Vasyl. «Individual and Calendar Memorialistic Rituals in Hutsulshchyna.» Scientific Bulletin of Uzhhorod University 2 (2021): 123-133.

17. Kilar, Anastasiia. «Memorial Motifs in Calendar Ritual Practices of Pokuttia Ukrainians (based on materials from Grodenky and Sniatyn districts).» Ethnographic Notebooks 1 (2017): 233-245.

18. Koval-Fuchylo, Iryna. «Lamentation in the Context of Funeral Ritual.» Folk Art and Ethnography 1 (2000): 33-44.

19. Koval-Fuchylo, Iryna. «Funeral Ritual: The Problem of Functioning and Perception.» Berehynia 1 (2000): 53-56.

20. Kostiuk, Lesia. «Memorial Rituals in Eastern Halychyna in the Second Half of the 20th – Beginning of the 21st Century.» Ukraine-Europe-World. International Collection of Scientific Works 11 (2013): 296-301.

21. Kutelma, Kornelii. «Folk Calendar.» Hutsulshchyna: Historical and Ethnographic Research. Kyiv: Naukova Dumka, 1987. 290.

22. Kutelma, Kornelii. «Polissian-Carpathian Parallels in the All-Ukrainian Calendar-Ritual Sphere.» Ethnographic Notebooks 3-4 (1994): 328-337.

23. Kutelma, Kornelii. «Ancient Basis in the Calendar-Ritual Practices of the Carpathian Ukrainians.» Ethnographic Notebooks 4 (1995): 204-208.

24. Levynovska, Liudmyla. «Mapping of Burial and Memorial Rituals in Pokuttia.» Bulletin of Precarpathian University. History 20 (2011): 238-246.

25. Nebesna, Zoriana. «Funeral Traditions of Ukrainians in Boykivshchyna at the End of the 20th – Beginning of the 21st Century.» Ethnic History of the Peoples of Europe 30 (2009): 59-64.

26. Pankiv, Mykhailo. «Mamko My, Zozulenko My...» Berehynia 1 (2002): 37-54.

27. Pankiv, Mykhailo. «Modern Traditional Rites in Pokuttia and the Problem of their Preservation.» Ethnos and Culture. Journal of Precarpathian University named after V. Stefanyk 1 (2003): 32-37.

28. Samotys, Yaroslav. Memorial Motifs in Spring Rituals of Ukrainians. Lviv: Institute of Folklore NAS of Ukraine, 2014. 16.

29. Siletskyi, Roman. «Memorial Motifs in Building Rituals of Ukrainians.» Ethnographic Notebooks 3 (2001): 479-482.

30. Sushko, Valentyna. «Perceptions of Death and Burial Customs of Hutsuls.» Folk Art and Ethnography (2014): 91-98.

31. Ulyanovska, Svitlana. «Ideas about the Spiritual Essence of a Person in the Context of Funeral Rituals.» Folk Art and Ethnography 3 (1989): 34-40.

32. Fitsak, Inna. «Funeral Traditions of the Inhabitants of Precarpathian Cities in the 20th Century.» Ethnic History of the Peoples of Europe 27 (2008): 89-93.

33. Tsyhanyuk, Olha. «Ritual Games in Funeral Customs of Ukrainians.» Ethnographic Notebooks 5 (1998): 646-647.

34. Cherleniak, Ivan. «Burial-Memorial Rites of Ukrainians in Zakarpattia at the End of the 19th – First Half of the 20th Century.» Notes of the Historical Faculty 27 (2016): 197-221.

35. Yakovleva, Olha. «Afterlife in the Imagination of Ancient Ukrainians.» Folk Art and Ethnography 2 (2005): 78-85.

36. Yaremchuk, Maria. «Burial-Memorial Rites of Lemkos at the End of the 19th – 20th Century.» Student Scientific Bulletin 34 (2014): 3-5.

LIST OF USED SOURCES AND LITERATURE (in the original language)

I.   Sources

1.   Вовк, Хведір. «Етнографічні особливості українського народу». *Студії з української етнографії та антропології.* Київ: Мистецтво, 1995. 335.

2.   Гнатюк, Володимир. «Похоронні звичаї й обряди». *Етнографічний збірник.* Т.31-32, Львів: Наукове товариство ім. Т. Г. Шевченка, 1912. 131-424.

3.   Кольберг, Оскар. *Казки Покуття.* Ужгород: Карпати, 1991. 327.

4.   Кузеля, Зенон. «Посижінє і забави при мерци в українськім похороннім обряді». *Етнографічний збірник.* Т.121, Львів: Наукове товариство ім. Т. Г. Шевченка, 1914. 173-224.

5.   Кузеля, Зенон. «Українські похоронні звичаї й обряди в етнографічній літературі». *Етнографічний збірник.* Т.31-32, Львів: Наукове товариство ім. Т. Г. Шевченка, 1912. 133-202.

6.   Онищук, Антін. «Похоронні звичаї й обряди в селі Зеленици, Надвірнянського повіта». *Етнографічний збірник.*

Т.31-32, Львів: Наукове товариство ім. Т. Г. Шевченка, 1912. 231-252.

7. Свєнціцький, Іаріон. «Похоронні голосіння». *Етнографічний збірник.* Львів: Наукове товариство ім. Т. Г. Шевченка, 1912. 1-129.

8. Філарет, Колесса. «Вірування про душу й загробне життя в українській похоронній і поминальній обрядовості». *Етнографічний збірник.* Т.242, Львів: Наукове товариство ім. Т. Г. Шевченка, 2001. 7-82.

9. Франко, Іван. «Галицько-руські народні приповідки». *Етнографічний збірник.* Т.2, Львів: Наукове товариство ім. Т. Г. Шевченка, 1907. 300.

10. Шухевич, Володимир. «Гуцульщина». *Етнографічний збірник.* Т.4, Львів: Наукове товариство ім. Т. Г. Шевченка, 1904. 271.

11. Falkowski, Jan. *Północno-wschodnie pogranicze Huculszczyzny.* Lwów: Nakladem Towarzystwa Ludoznawczego, 1938. 105.

12. Kolberg, Oskar. «Pokucie», *Obraz etnograficzny.* Т.1. Kraków: W drukarni uniwersytetu Jagiellonskiego, 1882. 367.

II.   Literature

1.   Артюх, Ліда. «Поминальні страви на Поліссі (народний етикет)». *Полісся України: матеріали історико-етнографічного дослідження.* Львів: Інститут Народознавства НАН України, 1997. 316.

2.   Боян, Світлана. «Головні християнські свята календарного обрядового комплексу бойків». *Україна: культурна спадщина, національна свідомість, державність* 17 (2008): 492-500.

3.   Василечко, Леонід. *Стежками відлуння.* Івано-Франківськ: Нова Зоря, 2003, 286.

4.   Войтович, Надія. *Народна демонологія Бойківщини.* Львів: Сполом, 2015. 237.

5.   Галайчук, Володимир. «З духовної культури Богородчанщини: звичаї, вірування та повір'я, пов'язані із світоглядними уявленнями про смерть та померлих». *Міфологія та фольклор 3-4* (2010): 27-49.

6.   Глушко, Михайло. *Методика польового етнографічного дослідження: навчальний посібник.* Львів: ЛНУ імені Івана Франка, 2008. 288.

7. Гримич, Марина. «Старість. Смерть. Культура вшанування небіжчиків». *Народна культура українців: життєвий цикл людини*. Т.5, Київ: Дуліби, 2015. 432.

8. Гузій, Роман. «Похоронні звичаї та обряди». *Етногенез та етнічна історія населення Українських Карпат*. Т.2. Львів: Інститут народознавства НАН України, 2006. 589.

9. Гузій, Роман. «Зенон Кузеля – дослідник похоронної обрядовості українців». *Народознавчі зошити 6* (2000): 1012-1016.

10. Гузій, Роман. «Народні засоби полегшення процесу помирання». *Народознавчі зошити 3* (1998): 330-334.

11. Гузій, Роман. «Охоронні звичаї та перестороги, пов'язані з наближенням смерті: порівняльні розсліди». *Карпати: людина, етнос, цивілізація: науковий журнал з проблеми карпатознавства 1* (2009): 163-168.

12. Гузій, Роман. «Ритуальне оплакування померлих в похоронній звичаєвості українців Карпат». *Народознавчі зошити 6* (2000): 809-815.

13. Гузій, Роман. «Традиційні способи перепровадження померлого на кладовище в похоронній звичаєвості українців Карпат» *Народознавчі зошити 3* (2001): 528-531.

14.   Гузій, Роман. «Традиційні способи повідомлення про смерть у похоронній звичаєвості українців Карпат». *Народознавчі зошити 5* (1998): 693-696.

15.   Гузій, Роман. «Уявлення та вірування українців Карпат про персоніфіковану смерть». *Народознавчі зошити 6* (1995): 362-366.

16.   Іванчук, Василь. «Індивідуальні та календарні поминально-маністичні обряди на Гуцульщині». *Науковий вісник Ужгородського університету* 2 (2021): 123-133.

17.   Кілар, Анастасія. «Поминальні мотиви у календарній обрядовості українців Покуття (на матеріалах із Гроденківського та Снятинського р-нів)». *Народознавчі зошити* 1 (2017): 233-245.

18.   Коваль-Фучило, Ірина. «Голосіння в контексті похоронного ритуалу». *Народна творчість та етнографія 1* (2000): 33-44.

19.   Коваль-Фучило, Ірина. «Похоронний ритуал: проблема функціонування і сприйняття». *Берегиня 1 (2000):* 53-56.

20.   Костюк, Леся. «Поминальна обрядовість у Східній Галичині другої половини XX – початку XXI століття». *Україна-Європа-Світ. Міжнародний збірник наукових праць 11* (2013) 296-301.

21.	Кутельмах, Корнелій. «Народний календар». *Гуцульщина: історико-етнографічне дослідження*. Київ: Наукова думка. 1987. 290.

22.	Кутельмах, Корнелій. «Полісько-карпатські паралелі в загальноукраїнській календарно-обрядовій сфері». *Народознавчі зошити* 3-4 (1994): 328-337.

23.	Кутельмах, Корнелій. «Прадавня основа в календарній обрядовості українців Карпат». *Народознавчі зошити* 4 (1995): 204-208.

24.	Левіновська, Людмила. Картографування похоронно-поминальної обрядовості на Покутті. *Вісник Прикарпатського університету. Історія 20* (2011): 238-246.

25.	Небесна, Зоряна. «Поховальні традиції українців на Бойківщині наприкінці XX – на початку XXI століття». *Етнічна історія народів Європи 30* (2009): 59-64.

26.	Паньків, Михайло. «Мамко моя, зозуленько моя…». *Берегиня 1* (2002): 37-54

27.	Паньків, Михайло. «Сучасні традиційні обряди на Покутті та проблема їх збереження». *Етнос і культура. Часопис Прикарпатського університету ім. В. Стефаника 1 (2003):* 32-37.

28. Самотіс, Ярослав. *Поминальні мотиви у весняній обрядовості українців.* Львів: Інститут народознавства НАН України, 2014, 16.

29. Сілецький, Роман. «Поминальні мотиви в будівельній обрядовості українців». *Народознавчі Зошити 3* (2001): 479-482.

30. Сушко, Валентина. «Уявлення про смерть і поховальні звичаї гуцулів». *Народна творчість та етнологія* (2014): 91-98.

31. Ульяновська, Світлана. «Уявлення про духовну сутність людини в контексті поховальної обрядовості». *Народна творчість та етнографія 3 (1989):* 34-40.

32. Фіцак, Інна. «Поминальні традиції жителів міст Прикарпаття в XX столітті». *Етнічна історія народів Європи 27* (2008): 89-93.

33. Циганюк, Ольга. «Обрядові ігри в похоронній звичаєвості українців.» *Народознавчі зошити 5* (1998): 646-647.

34. Черленяк, Іван. «Поховально-поминальні обряди українців Закарпаття кінця XIX – першої половини XX». *Записки історичного факультету 27* (2016) 197-221.

35. Яковлєва, Ольга. «Потойбіччя в уявленні прадавніх українців». *Народна творчість та етнографія 2* (2005): 78-85.

36. Яремчук, Марія. «Поховально-поминальна обрядовість лемків кінця ХІХ – ХХ століття». *Студентський науковий вісник 34* (2014): 3-5.

APPENDICES

Appendix 1

Funeral in Hutsul Region

(This is a funeral at the cemetery of the village of Zhabie for
Andriy Andriyovych Khrapchuk, the builder of the current
church of the Assumption of the Blessed Virgin Mary in
Verkhovyna. The grave has been preserved to this day.)

Appendix 2

Hutsul Funeral

(Funeral of Vasilina Kharuk, whose coffin needs to be turned to fit through narrow doors.)

Hutsul Funeral

(Funeral of Vasyl Ignatiuk in the village of Brustury, Kosiv region.)